Wisdom for Life

A Journey of Abundance, Peace, Happiness and Fulfillment

These powerful words are needed to live lively

Shivanakere Basavalingappa

Translated by

Prof. M. Basavaraj

INDIA · SINGAPORE · MALAYSIA

ISBN 979-8-89446-395-7

Dedicated to:

All those Vishwa-Bandhus (Universal Kins) who will read and adopt these principles and emanate these principles for the Loka Karunya (universal compassion)

Wisdom for Life

A Journey of Abundance, Peace, Happiness and Fulfilment

by: Shivanakere Basavalingappa

Secretary Karuna Jeeva Kalyana Trust (R.),

#2792, Shankar Plaza, 2nd Floor, 3rd Cross, 3rd Main Road, MCC 'B' Block, Davangere-577004

email: karunatrustdvg@gmail.com

Translated by:

Prof. M. Basavaraj

C-10, Vidyanagar,

Davangere-577005

Ph: 08192-260403, Mobile: 8095922202

email: basavarajmdvg@yahoo.co.in

Contents

The Swamiji's Blessings

Life is not a stagnant water. Stagnant water is the root cause for many diseases. In this background the Sharanas, saints and social thinkers with the noble intention that life should become full of health have left behind the pearls of wisdom of their life's experience for us. If only we understand and try to put them into practice it is possible to attain fulfilment in life. On this basis Sri Shivanakere Basavalingappa who always wishes only the good has gone on sending such pearls of wisdom through WhatsApp to us and also to thousands of people every day. If only we understand and try to put them into practice it is possible to attain fulfilment in life. Basavalingappa has gone on rendering pro-life service activities with love and compassion through 'Karuna Jeeva Kalyana Trust'. It is his policy that we should love even those who hate us. Love, tolerance, laugh, cooperation are a very huge capital of his life. He is endowed with the quality of reading and causing to read the rare works. His quality of tolerance and patience is appreciable indeed. He has limitless hope in life. He keeps reiterating that God has blessed a hundred years to man; one should make use of those hundred years meaningfully and fruitfully to the brim. He is always telling that we have come to this world "NOT for grudging enmity or keeping vengeance for a long time; but instead for achieving with love and kindness". He has captured and kept the pearls of wisdom which are complementary to that achievement in this small book. The very name he has given to this book is exciting. Verily in tune with the title word fulfilling Co-Journey of happiness and Abundance. These powerful words are needed to live there are drops of nectar in the small and tiny articles here. We would like to bring only a few of them to the attention of the readers. 'Several successful individuals too who having suffered and experienced sorrow, grief, pain, disappointment more than us and fallen into the abyss of the lower world have risen up like the phoenix. It is only such great achievers who have created history.' 'Let the pithy phrase try and try again always be our hymn or mantra' 'Let life throw whatever stones. May you build the bridge from out of them only. Don't you ever give up your firm resolve'. You are the one who knows better about yourself. None other than yourself. You please have lot of compassion on yourself. 'We ourselves are our severe critics. To think that we are not fit for kindness is a great self-betrayal'.

'The key of forgiving is in the heart. Forgiving is from the heart only and not from the mind.' 'Anger, hatred, jealously make us old hags much earlier besides making us ugly both internally and externally.' 'Let us die to the past immediately and bury them to create a new history'. 'The real spiritual value means it is knowing thyself only. Ever becoming a new person preserving liveliness all through itself is wisdom.' 'The culture of our family, its background and the environment we grew up under become the cause for our choices.' 'The gossip ruins the lives, slanders the name, breaks the families, spoils the friendship, kills businesses like cancer.' In every small-small articles too that are there in this book there is the quality of causing to be a great achiever if we read seriously, carefully and apply them in his life. There is no gap between Basavalingappa's life and his articles written here. In him there is the rare quality of instilling inspiration through his words talks and deeds. His untiring optimism is appreciable indeed. He does not believe in impossible. He has immense belief in the maxim "Where there is a will there is a way". He who says "Let us save water, let us grow trees, let us receive the grace of the mother nature" has been working to see that all his dreams come true. He is the one who always stands for at any cost and efforts to mitigate and eliminate the pains and sufferings of the distressed. All the words that are here emanate at this base point only. We wish that may these fill inspiration to the readers, cause to increase their zest of life in them and cause to kindle pro-life concern in them.

– Sri Panditharadhya Shivacharya Swamiji

Keeping Steps with This Work...

At birth man's nature will be characteristically that which is natural to an animal. It is only when man starts living as a social being he gets accustomed to the characteristics of a social being. In the journey of life it becomes inevitable for us to develop contact and companionship with many individuals. So much so that he who says that he can live outside society must be either a 'dog' or a 'god'. As a corollary of this societal living man comes in contact with both good and bad men alike. All of them do exert influence on us. If we go on accepting and embracing everything our personality becomes a nest of confusion. In this chaos 'we' get lost, When we face challenges the wisdom as to which part or factor of this our hotchpotch or the admixture personality we should use will not be there. Therefore in order to cause the life of peace and serenity to be ours we will have to cause our personality to be strong. Among the experiences that we face and pass through in life we will have to develop the capacity to discern which one we should accept for our personality development and with the same sense of humility which one we should reject. The pearls of wisdom which Basavalingappaji has collected and given here lend light to this kind of our thoughts; to that we have accepted to be right they lend justification through explanations, examples and the tales of experience. We have to be grateful for him for this.

That which is called life is no punishment. That is a gargantuan power which is bestowed on us. Living ever keeping on loving life is the way to keep that power enhancing. 'Love thy neighbour' is the preaching of the bible. Its another preaching 'Love thyself' is also there. Loving ourselves is not only right, it is also absolutely essential, says the bible. This kind of self-love will be composed of safeguarding our health, self-respect and self-value only and not rearing selfishness, jealousy about others, hatred etc. If this should become possible we have to see the life that we experience from different angles. Along the path we traverse ourselves personally that which becomes visible is only that which is caught by our eyes.

But the maxims which Basavalingappaji has culled out and given and in his explanations the footprints of several great achievers too appear to us; to start with it is enough even if they are followed earnestly, if there is promptness they will become ours too just as you keep seeing; afterwards the footprints that get imprinted become our own; perhaps they will become the beacon lights for those who come following us.

We read the maxims and forget them. After gathering and picking up the spread and scattered pearls one by one and string them by a thread that becomes a beautiful necklace. He has done that task. The pearls of wisdom that are here teach how to love life, not to run away from that. This is why and how they are the drops of nectar which give liveliness even in today's modern competitive life. For several maxims here Basavalingappaji's unique definitions being there is to be seen. The philosophy of being pro-life and optimistic that is here attracts us.

If looked that way, not many years have passed since G.C. Basavalingappaji of Karuna Jeeva Kalyana Trust was introduced to me. Need not pass either. It is because in the first meet itself his mild nature of winning the mind and friendly policy by which one is cleanly bowled over are his distinguishing features. Even afterwards too we both after exchanging our ideas and thoughts about our mutual works and activities have been benefitted. The pro-life activities which he has been doing through this Trust could be done by none but a selfless person like him. Hence, he is very dear to me. The present book which he has created and given is such a people-useful work that every writer too wishes that 'it would have been fine had I done it'. The readers will accept this with gratitude, like me.

– Prof. M. Abdul Rehman Pasha,
Bengaluru

The Writer's Words

The matters found here were by chance or somehow with me--either from the net or from friends. While searching some book these matters were found in zerox. Then itself reading some of them for sometimes, feeling happy I read them entirely and finished their reading. It neither had any captions, titles nor headings. Since the matters found here touched the heart, patted and enthused the mind in several dimensions, since felt that they were the words which should be followed I translated them from English to Kannada. Then giving it the title "Fruitful Co-journey of Jubilance and Abundance", I went on giving an apt heading to each topic. The translation of each and every topic too gave me great joy and delight. If the same joy and the good-hearted feeling that we should follow this virtuous topic comes to the readers too, it amounts to you, the esteemed readers, having given immense value to my small labour of love. While transforming the form if the Vachanas, Mankuthimmana Kagga, maxims or something else that was complementary to that topic which was in my heart flashed to my mind joining them too to this here and there and knitting them together into a beautiful necklace I have ventured to render a small service.

As for me in tune with the adage "For those who will have given birth even if the begotten baby be a bandicoot it looks beautiful and cute, to those who will have come together even if one partner is a monkey it looks beautiful to the other partner" this work of mine sounds dear and cute to me. The gracious-hearted readers themselves deciding this and taking it for what it is worth should raise and stud it in their crown. Here a confusion confronted me. Its writers, publishers are not known to me. I have not taken their permission. Is it right to bring this to Kannada...? At that critical time those that came to my help were two ideas_ "Knowledge is nobody's property. If these writings which are pregnant with wisdom become useful to the people and to the larger number of people at that it is enough. Guided by this yardstick I have Kannadised.

Once an admirer of Kuvempu brought an instance of plagiarism to the notice of Kuvempu (very well known kannada writer) by writing to him thus: "Some X has been writing your those writings after stealing them. You should take action against him". Quite interestingly Kuvempu is reported to have reacted to that laughingly saying: "Am I less accused? I have stolen from Pampa, Ranna, Janna. (Famous ancient kannada writers) He has stolen from me. That's all. Knowledge is an animate thing which keeps on moving. It is just enough if good thoughts become an inspiration to good deeds. It has no bindings. My hand is in Pampa's pocket, another's hand is in my pocket".

Chennai's Theosophical Society publishes the best magazine related to environment and humanism called "Wake up India" once in three months. In its first page itself its editor has requested that any of you can freely reprint and translate the matters of this magazine. No need of our permission. If it is brought to our notice we will be happy.

Do the service of causing to reach these to thousands and thousands of people. This brought and gave me still more courage and moral strength. Well now a couple of words about the matters that follow here.

The real riches, The power of abundance,

You excuse yourselves too,

Forgiveness is the foundation for release,

Daily you knowing yourself itself is wisdom, Life itself is power.

Like this there are 45 small, small matters in this book. The most important reason for this book to come in the print medium is the whisper of my conscience. It is my earnest wish that let this matter reach great many people, let them think it over and let them make their life golden.

Sanehalli's worshipful swamiji Sri Panditharadhya having immense love on me and these matters kindly wrote and gave the highly invaluable benediction words immediately. I offer my hearty gratitude to him.

I express my gratitude to the Notion press Chennai for agreeing to publish this book. And the translator Prof. M. Basavaraj for contributing great efforts and time for this noble purpose. Thanks to the original great writers and Sri Ravikiran, Proprietor, the Davangere Cement Concrete (It is my guess that it must be he who gave this matter in English) and to Karuna Jeeva Kalyana Trust's Assistant Manager Mrs. Veena Kumar who after typing the manuscript neatly correcting the mistakes here and there and brought this book to a shape in a short time. I am highly indebted to all of them.

Kindly read the activities of the Karuna Trust and do whatever possible financial assistance, guidance, cooperation etc., from you. The Karuna Trust will be most grateful to you.

It is an earnest appeal to the kind-hearted beings to know the pro-life, pro-people, constructive and altruistic activities of the Trust and charitably donate whatever possible amount to this account:

KARUNA JEEVA KALYANA TRUST (REGD.)
DAVANGERE

Account No. 50100332805356, IFSC: HDFC0000403
HDFC Bank Ltd. Davangere. Karnataka, India.
Email: karunatrustdvg@gmail.com, website:
karunatrust.co.in
Contact: 98866-45880, 8310520002
Please note that there is 80 g facility for the donors.

01

Real Riches

Think to experience the real riches. Cause the riches which can't be bought by money of your own. For example: nature, air, water, greenery, fellow beings, good relations, empowering conversations etc., are all real riches. There are hundreds of languages in the world. But "Smile" is the mother of them all. Smile can become the word of all languages. The word itself is knowledge. The word itself is ruby. It could be given, could even be kept too. The word could also cause it to fall, could build it too. As impossible situations wonderful opportunities come to all of us rather hidden or in disguise.

If we rot or decay in yesterday's defeats and repentances only, we will lose the sunrise, the sunset, the child's innocent smile, all the present love, happiness, joy and pleasure. If it is not possible to take up big, big works, shall we do small, small works themselves with pleasure? Let us start tasting and savouring the gifts of life fully right from where we are there at present. Illusion not required. Let there be the awareness of the actualities. One need not be a big man to start a constructive work. But to start "it needs a big mind", that's all!!! Many people thinking that "let all the conditions, finance, auspicious time etc., get set right the project, let us start thereafter". People just keep on waiting. Such of them just keep on and on till they die. They are no achievers.

To put the first step the end of the road need not be seen. It is not seen at all either. Saying "Let all the conditions set themselves right, we shall start after that" never ever keep waiting. Start immediately. Keep the conditions under your control. Importantly may we after developing our mind on the basis of the positive attitude found in the above words make the life a journey of supreme happiness and supreme fruitfulness.

02

Life's Challenges

In the every day life rows and rows of challenges come. Every week hollow-heap, difficulty-delight, pain-pleasure will all be there. Every human being though there is ever bright day time drowns and gets up in the absolute darkness of negativities like sorrow, disappointment, un interestedness.

All of us assuming that now the time is not good, it is not happening as we expected are dependent on time and circumstances. The incongruity or the adverse and unfavourable condition of circumstances will always be there. When felt so that which we could possibly do is one and the only course of action--we should keep on and on "trying, trying, trying again, trying once again". Only then we will understand one undeniable truth. Here and there several successful individuals who after suffering more grief, sorrow, pain, disappointment than us fell into an abyss have risen up like a phoenix. It is only such people who are the great achievers who created history. May the dictum "Try and try again" always be our hymn.

When somebody does a good or a virtuous deed congratulate him/her, express appreciation saying "Bravo'. Don't be resentful, envious and jealous. You continue your work with earnest effort. If someone is struggling in the flood of life "stretch a helping hand". You not only lend money and materials as help. Fill courage and fortitude. Then in your life too courage, fortitude and fruitfulness will be found on their own.

Irrespective of your level in relations in wealth, health and life-span you always be keen and ardent for your life's main purpose. Keep striving for it. Let the quality of putting forth earnest efforts repeatedly be in your every breath.

03

Just Heartily Involved in the Work

Just listening to your inner thoughts of wisdom start working. Without getting entangled in giving and taking just respond to the problems of others and help prevent and solve them. Help them transform their dream into a reality. When you need help unhesitatingly, putting the ideas of modesty, feeling ashamed out of your mind just ask boldly. The moment a mistake happens by you, own it and immediately ask to be excused. Just have an organic relation of cooperation with all, all living beings.

Just keep on growing.

Just try.

Just do the work you have taken up on hand consistently and persistently.

Do not give scope for the negative causes which tend the mind to postpone. Negativity is a bad condiment which produces a hot and burning taste in the mouth when eaten. When entangled in them try again and again and come out of those negativities. Always keep on learning the lessons of life personally and from the world. Come to the right path again and again. Start again, try again. By being a zero use the lever. Hoping like Archimedes that you can lift up the earth itself try and try again. Suffering, woe, struggle are all in the game. They are bound to be there. Take them sportively and by being a sportsman always be enthusiastic about your work and try again.

Let the life throw whatever stones at you. Build the bridge with verily with the same stones. Don't give up your firm resolve. If determination, incessant effort or attempt your highest ambition or desire is one of doing good to you and to all the living beings collectively never give up or backtrack. "Try, try, try". Never ever accept defeat in every matter, in every incident.

04

Kindness

The words of kindness will create and increase mercy, softness and self-confidence in both the speaker and the person spoken to. Kindness creates mercifulness, compassion in all living beings and the depth of softness in thoughts. The mercifulness in giving creates love. Kindness is there in all the fields of life. Follow and distribute that. Kindness is not one separate incident. It creates the waves of love, joy, sympathy every moment, moment after moment. It is a noun, an adjectival verb. It is many in one. Not just that much only. It is the natural highway of the joy and pleasure of life.

The society has taught the lesson that you should always be beware of and be careful about and guard yourself from the new peoples and the strangers. But if we don't have an open mind, if we don't open the heart we are sure to lose the invaluable secrets of joy and the contributions which are there in kindness. Mark my words: "There are no strangers in the world. Instead there is a friend who has not got introduced to or not become acquainted with. That's all." Let there be sympathy and kindness towards the strangers. Each one will be laden with his/her own load of sorrows. Let there be kindness aplenty towards your nearer ones too. We are knowing all about those who are nearer because they will be with us only. But let there not be this kind of indifference, callousness and intolerance. Those who are near us may go away from us any time; they may die. Let us respond to their feelings too. Kindness need not necessarily be big and lengthy. Many a time an act of small-small, natural – natural kindness does make the life's journey joyful and pleasurable. For example: A smile, a request to be seated, asking how do you do?... etc., which are acts of small mercies are in fact big gifts to others. Kindness builds an edifice of relations in strangers too. The relation that had existed becomes very much stable. It applies balm to the unnecessary misunderstandings that happen naturally. In this regard it is worth quoting Basavanna's words who said: "Will your wealth fly away if you say 'Why did you come, how do you do? Are you doing well? If you ask them to sit will the ground get dented to form a pit?"' First of all let there be mercy on ourselves. We only are our severe critics. It is a great self-deceit saying to ourselves that we don't deserve mercy or kindness, you yourself are your close and dear friend and your own enemy too. The best gift that we give to ourselves is mercy or kindness. We will be giving it to ourselves daily and incessantly. This is absolutely essential. Keeping the mind under control which always wants to get something or the other from others let we ourselves always give the light of mercy or kindness instead. Kindness does not mean only giving in kind or the giving of some material things. It could also be in the form of love, pardon, good conduct, humility, donation of time, donation of knowledge etc., that are not visible to the eyes. They too have great importance. When a material thing is given that thing becoming absent from you it becomes the donee's. "Knowledge, love, mercy are a fountain of nectar which causes to grow, increase and prosper both the donor and the receiver in a vigorous way. The principle of kindness. This bond is quite big. Kindness is a fascination of all living beings, which is dependent on both the inactive and the active elements." For example: Nature, father – mother, teachers, animals-birds, lastly a bacteria which is not seen to the eye too do give what all contributions to our large society of living beings! Merciful acts though howsoever small are not a waste. From the purity of inner mind or compassion the increase of joy, from the fruitful work-providing food come supreme love, supreme peace, supreme self-confidence and supreme fruitfulness.

05

Attitude of Good Determination

Our being associated with virtuous persons and by the influences we come under an attitude of good determinations is created. Don't spend much of your time in unrelated and unconcerned matters. If you don't give opportunities to the narrow and negative voices more time for the most valuable matters will definitely be available. We should not join with the commoners and the crowd. If we join with them we will not grow. We will grow where there is more of an atmosphere of the company of virtuous persons, virtuous determination, virtuous thinking and virtuous acts.

Always keep asking the following questions to yourself:

I am with whom?

In which way they are exerting influence on me...?

What do they tell me to read?

Which thoughts do they provoke from me?

More importantly, what do they want me to become? Afterwards let us ask a big question to ourselves. That if it is O.K.?

06

The Excusing Heart

The key to excuse is in the heart, excusing is from the heart only and not from the mind. When a thought comes about a person or on seeing that person if negative feelings arise it only means that we have not excused him/her. If contemplated some five minutes heartily as to what if we were in that person's position, then we may get kindness about what that person might probably have done. When said excusing from the heart it does not mean either that what all that person has done is right or that the way he/she has done is right. Our beliefs, values, ways-means may be completely different from theirs. "Excusing means only seeing the events from different dimensions and not that our perspective alone is right". Real kindness is a human experience. It is only from that experience itself all excuses should originate.

Kindness is love having no pity or compassion which does not involve sticking on to any infatuation. A clear life policy of seeing others impartially. A clear life policy of stopping the judging of other's acts and seeing with love. Besides it is a reaction of taking the responsibility about the processes explaining those acts in tune with my interest, opinions at will. If we keep on judging all the events that take place in life in terms of right or wrong, good or bad, there won't be gratitude at all about the challenges which life gives.

Be it a great leader, a philosopher, a saint, howsoever mature a person might be physically, mentally and emotionally the circumstances of challenges will always keep on coming. Nevertheless if we are not ever grateful to the invaluable lessons that those challenges bring, apart from losing the joy we will always become the victims of circumstances.

For example when Gandhi got pushed out from the train at midnight in the darkness at South Africa, if he were a negative or a pessimistic man thinking that he was a victim his life's aims, objectives and ideals would not have taken shape, let alone being materialized. And also the point of time of the freedom struggle of India might have been postponed still further.

07

You Excuse Yourself Too

Once we realize the truth it is easy to come out of pain, anger, intolerance, heatedness etc., we take the right decision. If we are obsessed with the mental attitude that "Only I am right", then anger will come, it is very much challenge to come out of these. It is because we will kill ourselves in these only. If we quit them it becomes easy to bring down the load off your shoulder. In the process of excusing importantly excusing yourself too is as very essential as excusing others. For many people it is easier to excuse others. But excusing themselves is rather very difficult.

Among the following or in any other matters you excuse yourself. When people cause pain to you, be grateful to them that you got an opportunity to excuse them. For having blamed others in the absence of clarity, when committed a mistake without owning responsibility for your acts you excuse yourself. For having got angry on others, for having felt jealous excuse yourself. Please forgive yourself for not having self-confidence in your strength and capacities to excuse yourself. First you excuse yourself for not having loved you accepting you as you are. Afterwards you respect yourself by only loving you, yourself and be grateful for however you are.

If you excuse yourself your life will really become joyful. There after you will see changes in all the fields. If looked that way what we think that itself gets realized in our life. Excusing does not at all mean that the excused person deserves it. But escaping from unnecessarily carrying that weight till we die and suffering from the mental torture and being comfortable is more important. Anger, hatredness, jealousy cause us to become old men much before we ought to be so. Along with that they make us ugly both internally and externally. In making you love yourself more and respect yourself more "Excuse" or "Pardon" plays a very decisive role. You will keep and treasure this gift with you generously, won't you...?

08

Blame – Pain are Mutually Equal

The speed and haste with which we get our mental pain and agony also are in direct proportion to the speed and haste with which we jump to blame others. While keeping on blaming the outer enemies we become the enemies to ourselves. Instead let us follow Basavanna's very psycho-diagnostic Vachana (a rhythmical prose composition which runs like a metrical verse):

> Those who blamed me I call them my father and mother
>
> Those who scolded me I call them relatives
>
> Those who ridiculed me I call them my born relatives
>
> Those who praised me I call them they hanged me on golden hanging.
>
> Those who hit me I call them those who protected me.
> Koodala Sangamadeva.

If we follow this in toto we will become friends to ourselves by becoming the ones whose enemies are not yet born. Though all this is known to us the moment fear, unfavourable conditions occur we exhibit our bad conduct without our knowledge like a machine. Though the automatic habits, thoughts, reactions, feelings, emotions etc., that are there in our brain have been occupying our mind it is not necessary that we should react immediately. Usually in a few hours that follow after having got angry we feel repentant after becoming aware of our mistake. A feeling of remorse coupled with a sigh of relief makes us feel that it should not have happened like this. After the anger the cruelty transgressing not having even an iota of consciousness as to what we have been doing at that moment there have been quarrels, bickering, fighting with exchange of blows and even murders have taken place. All these finally end up in pain, agony, anguish, a sense of crime and punishment.

It is not necessary that we should live like this by we ourselves making us the mental prisoners. But, alas, bound by the restrictions of our past memories we kill our beautiful future too by our own hands. What a pity that every day forgetting the joy, mirth, merriment, song, jubilant shout, laugh and light we push ourselves into a well of darkness. We know pretty well which is good for us and for others. We know higher life, thought, natural peaceful life. But in a fit and moment of anger we simply forget all of them. When our emotions are under control by our wisdom, this bad habit or tragedy will not happen. The choice is ours. Then the absolute darkness's difficult nights will elapse. Again the light of wisdom will dawn.

Everything is possible by self-control. Gandhiji's words that by self-control and self-confidence any type of achievement too can be achieved are true of all time and clime.

09

Forgiveness is the Foundation for Liberation

The very act of declaring the mental wounds and pains inflicted since a long time ago as "Let it be, leave it" is excusing. Excusing those who are felt to have done wrong and injustice and caused pain to us and also excusing us too is the best option for our mental peace. It does not mean a justification of the incident that has taken place. Instead let us excuse with a better and nobler purpose of making our mental life easy to be traversed in future and move forward towards a sublime future. Excusing means reselecting our life and strengths, getting up from the drainage of pain, taking bath and living in this present moment completely releasing from the lurch of the bygone past.

True. We all know it. Life means it is a series of many challenges. We all have experienced a series of trials and tribulations one after the other. Financial cheats, frauds and deceptions, dishonesty, disappointment in love, betrayal, losing of job, insults and humiliations, economic loss, diseases, accidents, violence, wars, deaths... etc. Like this the endless pains and sufferings of life will be at once excessive and unbearable. We will have chalked out the defensive techniques too to prevent and drive them out according to time and circumstances.

By transferring our pain to the concerned or the society we immediately take a palliative tablet for instant relief. Thinking that "Mine is right, yours is wrong. But then should it happen to me only?" We try to find solace by saying god, destiny, fate, sin of previous lives. In order to run away from the pain saying 'Ayyo'...!!! for the immediate mental release making somebody, something responsible or blaming oneself saying that "I myself is responsible" feeling deep sorrow we make our life miserable and a virtual hell. But the simple beautiful truth means by complaining no use or benefit resulting from that but instead the problem gets still more aggravated. The way to come out of that itself not being there we ourselves get self-imprisoned in the dark room. It is only a temporary comfort or solace but it won't solve the problem. The pain remaining inside in as it is, that pain actually keeping on growing longer that pain itself gets harder again and again. By ruminating the past time and the painful events again and again we experience now exactly as much pain as we experienced then. This circle getting repeated again and again the pain goes on increasing. Anger and the feelings of abusing will keep on coming. We feel that getting angry, determining to maintain hatred and enmity and to take revenge, tit for tat, eye for an eye, tooth for a tooth is our right or self-sympathy, self-violence, helplessness will continue. If so what should be done generally does not get to be known at all. "The one and the only expedient plan means excusing. May mercy or kindness, friendship always be there on you and on others."

Only excuse is the remedy for this vicious circle. Only that is the balm for incidents of pain of the past. It is the firm foundation for internal peace of mind and the sublime life of the future after getting released from the burden, pressure and unnecessary works. For many people all this is known. All these will have come in the moral stories of childhood. But still despite the past experience and though having the will to excuse excusing is very difficult. That how to excuse too will not have been known. "Let us remember. Excuse will not change the past. It builds the future." Let us sing a requiem to all the events of the past today itself and create new history. Pains are inevitable. But to undergo suffering and to feel the pain is optional.

The weakness of not excusing causes to make the daily life a hell. It is a jail constructed by ourselves only. It is a small room. By the negative self-inflicted violence the physical and mental diseases getting increased it will not at all be possible to live "in the present moment".

10

Daily Knowing Myself Itself is the Wisdom

The real spiritual value means "You knowing yourself itself". Always keeping on becoming a new person retaining or preserving the liveliness itself is wisdom. By the events of the past what all decisions we may have arrived at figuratively dying in relation to all of them we should start our life de novo (afresh) saying "I should know myself". No theories are required for this. Different Theory, Dvaita (duality), Advaita (non-duality) theories too are not required. Keeping all these aside keeping on reviewing our life ourselves let us get ready for a better life in future. This requires a sense of detachment about results/consequences and knowing the truth deeply. This is not possible for those who have a weak heart. This is possible only for those who have a fearless will keeping aside fear and sorrow. It is at once, a challenge and an invitation for us to become physically, mentally and emotionally mature and perfect. Keeping aside the process of knowing by others, by books, we require the state of awakening of 'I knowing myself'.

The devotional song of Buddha, Basava, Gandhi is not enough. Knowing ourselves we too should achieve. Knowing the self is not a zerox copy of another person. It is a state of consciousness. It is a process of delving deep into the depth of inner awareness keeping on increasing the capacity of I myself getting to see my truth. It is an experience of becoming one, becoming one with the totality. It is a soul-cantered perspective which keeps on evolving by perfection and maturity crossing all borders and frontiers after leaving all that we know. It is leaving "I, mine" and embracing a much wider conception of "We, ours"; the feeling that it is of the entire community of the living beings is important. It is a firm and brave journey of the experiences of nectar called "It is the right of all". Keeping on giving both humility and ecstasy or supreme happiness it is the inaugural ceremony of the life's journey of peace and fruitfulness. Walking out from the theories propounded by others itself is a big challenge. We only should awaken and arouse our knowledge or awareness and wisdom. As a complementary to this we should develop a virtuous wisdom that "By this thought, word and by this act/work is it going to be good to me and to the world. Self knowledge/awareness is not that easy. Externally, internally the seed of ego dying away, the process of causing to grow the tree of supreme happiness of the individual and of the world along with the effects happening in future too will be out of our reach at that moment. We should dissolve in our deep sleep our own world constructed by ourselves. The release of the bindings of all levels will take place in pleasant sleep. We should do the practices of supreme happiness, supreme peace and supreme fruitfulness.

11

Choices of Wisdom

If your hitherto choices have brought a feeling of dissatisfaction and imperfection in you, you instead of blaming your choices you should consider that your choices themselves are responsible for the problem. What all happen to you every day are the consequences of your choices of wisdom. We wrongly imagine that for the situations we are in now life, God, vaastu (building a building on astrological basis of Hinduism), fate are responsible. It is the supreme truth that for what am I today for that the choices of every day's good wisdom only are responsible. For our sorrow, for our dissatisfaction our choices of the past are only responsible but not those incidents.

For example, for the accident that happens in over-speed is our choice of over speeding is only responsible, the accident is in no way responsible. More than that incident the reactions are still more frightful. Response to a stimulus or reaction means the relief or solution as to what next remedy itself is important and not the choice of the past. It is of no use blaming the people and the condition behind that.

We hesitate to take up the achievements that seem laborious and unbelievable. The reason being putting all our blamings and complaints on others, on the world and the situation, not performing our duty, not using our power to do or capacity and will power and then slipping away smoothly. Truly speaking we should have to be responsible to our internal world only. To the thoughts, feelings, pains and desires we ourselves should be responsible. We will have thought that our joy, happiness, the quality of life are created by these internal thought choices. It is because "If there is clarity about what should not be done, what choice should be made, then the life will be one of security and happiness".

12

Intelligent Choices

Though all of us set our foot on this world in one and the same way. Only our end of life and the joys and pleasures in between are determined quite differently by the choices we make. By our choices they might become either the best friends or the worst enemies. For all that we have with us now are due to our choices only. All the day-to-day affairs of life like the success and failure, the profit and loss, the pros and cons have their roots in our choices. Every choice after some time gets transformed into a habit. If we don't make the right or proper choice apart from we remaining backward in life we may have to go on making only the tough choices in future too. Even if doing no choices you remain neutral and inactive then there will be a reward in accordance with that inaction. You make choices. The choices will build your life.

Whether every decision that we have taken is wise or otherwise, one of wisdom or of stupidity will shape our future life. As we sow, so shall we reap. Joining the college, leaving it, whom to marry?, whether the last drink is desirable or not before driving the car?, shall I speak negative words or not about another person?, shall I ring up the phone to my would-be customer or not? shall I say I love you or not...? Every choice like this does throw several good consequences or bad consequences on our life's causes and effects. The biggest challenge of all of us is that none of us choose bad choices consciously. The big problem means we make choices in our sleeping state. Without using wisdom, awareness we make choices negligently. For 50% of the people the awareness about what they are choosing will not be there at all. The culture of our family, the background, the environment or the atmosphere under which we will have grown will become responsible for our choices. They all will be so naturally adopted and well-knitted like the warp and weft of our daily life that they will all becoming natural habits. We will not be having any control over the choices at all. None of us will be desirous either to cause our belly to grow big and bulgy or to become a pauper or an insolvent, or to take a divorce. But generally the small and tiny bad choices getting multiplied will open the flood gates for this kind of bad effect and a difficult situation. We will have made this kind of a choice without a wishful thinking, analyzing and weighing the pros and cons before taking a decision. So long as we make choices devoid of consciousness they can never be good habits. As the seed, so the tree. By sowing a bitter neem seed you cannot hope to reap a sweet mango fruit! In the same way without following a good conduct it is not possible to bring better results. Now "after getting awakened and arisen" by being most vigilant to make choices that make our life quite strong and robust morning is the auspicious time. The choice made in a state of sleep is enough means enough. May you continue your journey towards your goal, towards your dream. In that case your journey is sure to continue from greatness to glory and from glory to grandeur.

13

Friendship and Compassion

Control not required. May there be friendship and **compassion**. When there is strong control over life there will be no chance or opportunity for love to make an entry at all. We, live like the tightly held fist, will not be in a state of pleasure and relaxed. Then we will be having haste; mental tension, strain etc, Without experiencing the jubilance, abundance, fruitfulness and lóve. we will be caught entangled in a control machine. In case you go on controlling the feelings and thoughts of your children, your parents, your servants or your own you will feel the tension inside you like a pressure cooker. We feel that we should control everything and everyone. Otherwise we feel that my existence will be in a jeopardy or great danger or the situation will not be under control.

Generally there will be fear about the grip over finance, too much of eating, the fear of the disease-related issues. There will be fear about the social behaviours or that what will happen in future. Exaggerating these, the mind continuously tries to keep these under control. It is because the mind does not know the act of loving life at all. It is largely under the control of the conditions of the past time.

The life of tight grip that we feel is just resistance. Besides our ego remains always powerful it will always be creating the control that only mine should be carried out.

Lastly the mind which is hell bent on controlling is itself highly fickle and inconsistent. This deep desire has been responsible for very big disbelief, quarrels and bickering right from the beginning of mankind down to this day.

The reason for this misunderstanding is the presumption I have presumed myself that I am powerless, the one who is not fit for love, the one who is cared by none and a disliked individual. I am the one who is blind, deaf and dumb to the love of the people of the world. There are many rational and logical reasons for all of us in our society to control our life. But still for many people it is not possible to come out of this control. It is because of the simple reason of not seeing for themselves the natural divine factors like the supreme happiness, the supreme love, the supreme peace, the supreme self-confidence and the supreme fruitfulness which are hidden in them.

We forget this sacred, omnipotent, omnipresent conscience power, love power very much being present in ourselves. The duality whether I should control or I should let free will be there very subtly or delicately in all of us. The society will keep on preaching us that you exercise control over the children, the family, the servants and all those you came in contact with to the extent possible.

Only for just a few lakhs of people in the world the truth that "Leave control, give liberty, repose trust in life" might have been fully convinced. Only a few who have trusted and reposed faith in life will become the free thinkers. The obstinate and an unyielding society having firm hold with its hand-fist sees and tries to control them. The person who does not control and who has the consciousness/sense of a free heart will be a source of infinite vigour, power and strength.

14

Unique Characteristics

Higher unique characteristics will not be there in an individual at his birth itself. Later on we develop the characteristics ourselves. Some of them will be very effective while some others will not be so effective. We who are conscious human beings can become more effective in our respective fields of work by developing higher qualities. The most important among them is talking positively about another person. Without this it is not possible to develop our personality well. Talking positively with another person will be helpful in building up that person's personality and to lift up and encourage that person. Some out of false pride assuming that they are the most honest and direct talkers exhibit more cruelty than being direct.

Positive talk about another not only creates the name of compassion and goodness but also creates an atmosphere of persuasion. It builds up their personality. But the negative words don't have this type of features at all. Humiliating words cause to bring down both the person who speaks and the person spoken to.

A folklore story of the 19th century "The wing and the feathers in the air" is like this. A city. There was a virtuous saint. A youth of that city was keeping on teasing, blaming and abusing the saint. The saint, for one, used to be not attached to worldly things, clam and unperturbed. One day the youth himself having realized his mistake asked forgiveness. Though the youth had asked the saint that he be forgivenessed the saint having felt that the youth has not properly realized his mistake put a condition for forgivenessing him. The saint said: "Tear the quills and feathers that are there in the pillow which is there in your house into rags and pieces, going to the top of the hill throw them into the air to fly away". Though this condition sounded rather strange to the youth he did exactly like that only. He felt happy that at last it was solved so easily. He then came back to the saint's house and asked: "Have you now forgivenessed me?" To that the saint told him to pick up all those quills and feathers again and come. The youth said that it was not possible at all since the wind has after carrying them wheresoever has thrown them away helter-skelter. "Likewise the bad words uttered by you too spreading throughout the market have created hatredness and intolerance", said the saint. Word is a ruby, is constructive. The words that are undesirable and unbecoming, the words that bring evil, the words that cause loss to others should never be distributed at all. They do have negative power. Actually there is nothing which is more harmful than this.

15

Gossip

Gossip destroys lives; brings bad name by defaming and causing damage. It breaks families; ruins friendship. It kills business, dealings and affairs like cancer.

Please see that which is positive instead of the negative words. Be committed to the skill of speaking positive words. Before speaking weigh the pros and cons that your words might bring about. Only speak the words which are favourable to others and to you. Shun gossiping. Gossiping is unnecessary. Please do speak only the positive words instead of the negative words. It might not be possible to put that into practice immediately or it might never ever be possible at all. But to what extent we use the positive words, we only derive enthusiasm, joy, peace, fruitfulness to that extent. We can earn strength or power from words. To create anything, it must first germinate as a thought after which only it comes into existence in words. It is only by the words we construct or we destroy. Though spoken in any language our will comes into existence by our words only. Your dream, feeling, what you are...that, all these come into being by your words only. Your word is a very big power. That by aiding communication, contact and expression greatly creates life's many positive events. Really word itself is a pearl, a ruby; a life giver. It is by word a joke or peels of laughter, again it is only by words of hatred, enmity, ill-will, impurity and filth, evil and virtuous deeds. The words have immense power. Positive words are twice-blessed--they bless those who say them and also those who listen. Positive words like appreciation, gratitude, wishing good to others bestow strength both to us and to them. If we use negative words like heatedness, intolerance, jealousy it causes loss of mental power to others and to us too. It is by using words we can either make others feel proud about themselves instead of getting weary, annoyed and dissatisfied about us. The choice is entirely ours.

We create many good and/or bad situations by words only. As leaders, as entrepreneurs there is a very big responsibility on us. A word is like a double-edged sword and it can cause and bring the development of the individual or it can also ruin him. Do make a firm resolve. When it is necessary to speak, you should definitely speak. But see whether it is going to be useful to you and to others by that. If it is not you better keep silent. Whenever it is possible speak positive only. It is definitely possible to be positive always.

16

Life

The life is a process which apart from limiting our limitations establishes its supremacy over our limitations. That which goes on increasing the consciousness of the wave lengths of living here and now at the present moment itself is life. Life is a very big power. It is no punishment. When the people do not achieve that which they would like to achieve feel for themselves that life is a punishment. If our dreams and expectations do not come into reality it only means that we have not discharged the necessary responsibility. The actual truth is that not having utilized the life's powers properly we have not got the fruit. Life is a power. Living too is power, you better know.

If any work, thought, is felt to be impossible we ourselves are responsible for that. The reason for our failures is not too far to seek. Not raising our consciousness level to the level of that work and not engaging or involving ourselves actively in that work itself is the reason for that. By empowering our level of consciousness quitting the negative attitude that it is NOT possible by us we can keep on expanding the fences of possibilities. If we raise our consciousness to the level of the tasks taken up, then nothing is impossible to us. Realizing this, if we live with that realization, keeping on changing our limitations, throwing away the bond of limitations which we ourselves had put we can build newer possibilities and successes.

By giving attention to this process we will be empowered by ourselves. From several generations of previous lives to the present one, by hereditary and genes and in the surrounding environment we get negative thinking that "we are small, dwarfs, pigmies and weak and powerless". Then we think we have meagre power. But the truth is entirely different. We should say to ourselves that we are "wise, dynamic and powerful.

On the power of truth we should stand on a firm resolve. When we refuse the lies to ride on us the negativities melt away just as the mist melts itself away as soon as there is the sunrise.

17

The Word Itself is Strength, the Word Itself is Death

In your words there is immense strength. Whatever and what all we do every day that itself will actually get a tangible form. If you talk with positive and proper or right words about others their strength increases. That will give strength to you also. If you talk negatively there will be loss of strength to them and to you too. By the strength of your word the others will fall at your feet in reverence or they might even cut your head. Please understand the power of words.

The words we speak, the thoughts we think and the feelings we entertain are our real strengths. These will certainly exert their own respective influence on us and on others as well.

18

The Power of Abundance

After finding out the purpose of life if we start working on it, that purpose itself brings abundance aplenty. Doing that which we love is the good objective of life. Then that contributes to the good of the world humanism in some way. Money becoming a by product, flows effortlessly from abundance. Listening the inner voice of the heart, following the whispers which come there, performing special work we should proceed. That work should be continued by doing propaganda too. It is absolutely essential. It is because let others too taking part in this service, get inspired as well. You better do only what is needed to you and to the society. Money will definitely come. Running behind or chasing after money is not required. Money gets attracted as if by a magnet through your works. Let our development of wealth be proved through the contributions we give to the society. By the growth of your spiritual power the power of abundance will grow profoundly. May you and your works be the convenors of that power.

19

Let Us Bloom Again and Become Children Again

As a child we came to this world by being completely free. We were in the womb without having the feelings of insecurity and fear and without being scared. Later on during our infancy and childhood being a fountain of incessant joy, our heart was imbued with natural, free, fearless happiness and pure love without any traces of impurity or blemish. We used to mix and mingle with all and everything continuously. When we were children the act of touching and getting touched was as natural as our breathing. Afterwards, throughout our childhood knitting a net itself of social restrictions we were tied up. A training was given as to how we should all adapt and adjust ourselves to the society. The fear of punishment was put as a string attached to the failure to adhere to this freedom. How to talk and how not to talk with the people in a manner agreeable to the society; how to behave and how not to behave with all in work, in play, amusement and studying and in everything was taught.

The social restrictions and constraints the "Do's" and the "Don'ts" putting control on the child's feelings, separating and isolating the child from others made the child aloof and far away from others. As if it is not enough this fear-based system threatened that it might have to punish those who violate these social laws. These rules are so deeply rooted in our brain that we unconsciously follow these every day, in fact day in and day out.

Nowthatyouhavebecomegrown-ups,knowledgeable and since you have got self-acquintance with facts like what is what, awareness and understanding, insight and discernment, you should get released from each of these imposed controls. Our life consists of mental, emotional, social and physical walls of jail. Coming out of that, enjoying the inner liberty and being free is of prime importance. Knock down and cause the walls to fall down, build bridges. You already pretty well know as to which rules curbing and suppressing your liberty put you in jail. We should know that the wind, light and the greenery of inner liberty is so much abundant, so much pleasurable and the one having plenty of liveliness and cheerfulness. Let us throw all the walls of rules into the wind. Not yielding to and not being cowed down by any restrictions and obstructions let us welcome the path of the heavenly pleasure of liberty.

The outer world is our playground. For the spiritual attainment of life the world is just mercury. All those who interact and intermix with us are the mirrors that reflect our inner-self or mind. The people behave with us in accordance with their inner feelings and thoughts.

With how much of a free, open mind, real compassion and love we deal with others, we get exactly that much of compassion, affection, love and sympathy from others too in our every moment's existence.

20

Life is Mysterious

We get thrown from one experience to another incessantly. One moment we have a feeling of excess, another moment we have joy, sorrow, vagueness, confusion and chaos. In this way only life gets going on and on. These oppositions are the challenges of divinity. These descending deep into the depth inside our inner self itself help us to get the answers. These true answers transforming all the questions will establish contact and communication to the existence of our heart. Then we will not be sticking on either to the good or to the bad or we will not deny that which is bad. We will not like either to wish that let only that which is good should happen or even to escape saying that something dreadful will happen. Something begins to happen in the miraculous point in between these two oppositions. This is a sweet and sacred vision of we seeing ourselves. Those visions of oppositions having the quality of being unaffected by external happenings like gain, loss, fear, joy, distress, disappointment etc., cohabiting with each other make to find out the existence together through harmony. Then a deep success comes about without any effort. Besides, life keeps on continuing in a right, in a proper equal weight of happiness in a state of an equilibrium.

Instead of you getting entangled again in the hook of negativity about you and about others you will carry on the flight of a free bird. This will be completely convinced to you by yourself. Such a man is free, really. Then he becoming soul-centric celebrating full freedom will be leading a life of jubilance, abundance and fruitfulness.

21

Be Vigilant About Your Thoughts

If we observe every thought that comes to us carefully we get full freedom in life. This cannot be done through control or negligence. This is possible through knowing whether the thoughts are positive or negative, will they create hatredness or have they been creating love. They are just thoughts only; some of them are positive while some of them are negative and still some are neutral. On the basis of how you react or respond to these thoughts you will become either the master or the slave. One who has achieved good relation with the mind should welcome every thought as if it is a new guest. We need to welcome the thoughts of wisdom with love, giving a cup of tea and make them divine. Now the thoughts will have got transformed as free gifts. These are really big gifts. All these thoughts are only subtle and delicate rules for spiritual awakening.

22

The Real Strength

We should observe the thoughts which weaken us many times during the day. During such moments giving several reasons for this situation we presume that there is no relief or solution for this with us. Along with the worries confusions too getting started we give colour to them. Then frustration getting to grow, fears enclosing us from all sides we ourselves will get imprisoned in our own mind's jail.

Owing to those limitations we have to undergo the punishment. To call ourselves weak whosoever did whatever or did not do is not the reason. For the feeling of weakness what did whatever or did not do is not the reason either. The present situations and conditions too are not the reason. The real strength means believing that the power to do what is required to be successful at this moment and to attain what desire we have is already within us.

The real power, after lifting us up from the situations of challenge, frees us from the fears and the thoughts of yesterday and tomorrow which give us trouble. Strongly believing that what all situations come, whatever they may be they are for our good only is most important.

Definitely that power is very much within us. By changing weakness into a feeling of strength we can lead our life easily, smoothly, happily and successfully in accordance with our desired purpose without any pressures, sufferings and agonies.

23

Success

When we hear the success story of someone, we just see only the achievements. But we are blind to the fact that they too will have experienced the trials and failures, disappointments, losses and failures and the days of agony in their life.

Nobody, we and they too are perfect. They too and you too pass only after failing. We should grow only by keeping on learning and becoming stronger. Foundation is the basis for achievement. Only intensity will creates the highest achievers. We should become the most dissatisfied ones. Those who have the dissatisfaction of the lowest or the least level are the defeated ones.

24

Forgiveness

Forgiving is "The gift you give to yourself". That will release us from our past bitter experiences and bring back previous relations. That will facilitate "to live in this present moment". Only when we forgiveness ourselves and others we are really the free individuals. By forgiveness we will definitely get terrible freedom.

Many a time without forgiving ourselves raking up the painful experiences again and again we cause the wound and cancer. So, you love and forgiveness yourselves and the others too. It is because life will be going on "only at this moment". Then the old bitterness, the past pain descending from your shoulder flee away whereby your heart becomes wider. If you come from the sky of love you are always safe. Forgive today itself and now itself. Forgiving yourself. Forgetting the old bitter and sweet experience savour life becoming a totally new person whose newness never existed before. The most powerful power means it is learning "the art of forgiving" well.

By keeping on intollerence of ill-will and hatred in a measure small or big against someone, getting heavy weight, be it small or big, glued to the heart we cause to weaken our physical and mental power by suffering unnecessarily. This will create adverse effects or evil consequences in several fields at several stages of our life.

If we entertain anger, bitterness, disappointment, frustration on others for many days that will burn our own selves. If we keep the pains of insults and humiliations on our chest it will not only ruin our power but also ruin our future by the memories of the past time. Besides it attracts verily that type of a negative person and the events.

You will do well to remember that "worry is the interest we pay for the troubles we imagine".

25

By Healing Self-Freedom

Forgiving creates self-freedom to us, a present for healing up. Our personality gets ripened by this. If we are in pain we give pain to others too. If we ourselves are in enjoyment we give enjoyment only.

If another person does not accept your forgiveness it is a loss to him. You, for one, will be free from pain. Though some keep vengeance of obstinacy or stubbornness, enmity, hatredness, quarrelling till they die they will undergo as much mental pain. Our job is forgiving; dying for the events of the past. Believing that in god's creation and way everything is alright and to live accordingly.

Nature, the world never ever commit mistakes. Everyday there will be many opportunities of quitting our ego and inviting love. Or saying "'Mine itself is correct' obstinately sticking to our gun that our wrong itself is right we can suffer too unnecessarily". Every moment we have the freedom to choose forgiveness. Without offering resistance the choice of being comfortably free from worries, distresses and sorrows is entirely ours. Forgiving continuously is a process of forgiving forever. "If we bury the past events we will cause to make the light feeling, the body which is light, a life without obligation and the word without enmity or ill-will our own, we get freedom".

26

Healing Creates Happiness and Comfort

If after our pains heal up and vanish and joy is filled up in us what we want is materialized. If we keep less resistance, less fear, less of a great desire in life that we want will naturally flow to us.

Stepping down to the depth of the mental, physical and the emotional wounds that come to us we should treat them ourselves. If we invest the capital of time to that naturally we will come out of those wounds and we also get the higher spirituality too at the earliest. By the firm resolve to come out of the devil of the past time and the necessary actions the mind becomes free.

If we get released ourselves about 100% from our past time, the ego which makes us struggle and our way difficult and to undergo sufferings will loosen its hold on our life. "The ego in the illusion of the seeming or the apparent truth always showing the sleight of its hand will always be getting on to and sitting on our shoulders." Nevertheless "through forgiving and the process of healing the ego could be subdued and forced to bend in reverence". By attaining contact with the nature of everlasting abundance we can attain divinity.

Without leaving saying "I" the self story of should it happen to me only...? growing in degree and growing stronger, getting entangled in the story of the feeling of having become a scapegoat we undergo intense suffering. Even before forgiving itself the obstinacy of ego catches hold of us in its vice-like grip without we becoming aware of it. This is the last caution bell of the impending danger. It is because the ego never ever wishes to die. It won't give out its old stories.

The stories of the past themselves are the abundant basis for the survival of ego. If said leave out ego the scapegoat which is felt right to us growing stronger the mind begins another new big game. After releasing the ego of small and minor wounds we should chop off the fascination or fondness of all of its expectations, wants and desires. Instead of that "after choosing trust and a state of surrender, always sharing with others the creativity of the boundless limitless love which is with us is the 'Sanjeevini' (a herb supposed to make a dead person come alive) of life."

27

Life is Not a Struggle

The purpose of life is not to struggle. When we resist life, when we struggle, then life too becomes struggle filled.

"Your life's perspective is a very big companion in your life. It causes you to know your thoughts, how is your life. Your thoughts themselves will determine your future. You yourself will choose the sweetness, pleasantness or the deliciousness and the tune of your song. Your life is always loyal and faithful to your thoughts. Life will not struggle against us. We ourselves will struggle against life.

What seed we sow that itself will sprout. Of what avail is blaming the sprout out of foolishness? Of what avail is blaming the world? As I am, as are my thoughts so is my world: all of us conceive and make a mental image that our life should be like this only.

We wish that our life should be so built as we build it by putting force. When that which we wanted that it should be like this only did not happen like that, wishing that the future should happen like this only when all these did not happen, holding our fist tight, holding our breath we start the struggle.

In order to accept life as it is it needs maturity, experience and wisdom; not acceptance, inaction and cowardice. All of us, naturally wish that the things should go on as we wish them to go on.

In reality, though wishing to live as a realist we don't live like that. The moment we get disappointed we hold our fist tight. "Life is infallible, never commits mistakes. Life in fact guides us. Be free from illusion and ruthlessly frank, don't get stuck or attached. Like this life will keep on giving the message. If we act always by being positive whatever that is due to us will definitely come to us". Life flows, we too should flow with it.

28

The Light of the Universe

I have come from the light of the universe

I am born as a human being by the lover of the universe

I have become a granary of power by getting the power of the universe.

I have risen from the heart of the universe

I command to myself that I am a universal kinsman

I am living in an endless abundance. "The endless abundance of the universe is the origin of the source of my life". The river of my life will never stop flowing. It is flowing as a manifestation through me.

Let us believe that which is good is coming in an unexpected and a surprising way and God is blessing me.

I am now praying with an open heart for the coming of God. "There is nothing which is better than the truth". Anything which is still more surprising need not happen to me.

"Since I myself am the source of the birth of the universe, since all the essential factors that are present in the universe are very much in me only, nothing is surprising to me". I am not the one carrying the burden of the thoughts of the past time and of the future. The past has gone. The future has not yet come. Yesterday is no more, tomorrow is not yet born. So, act in the living present. Yesterday is history. Tomorrow is a mystery. Today is a gift. That is why we call it "the present..."

On the basis of my beliefs and along with the deliberate fearless works I keep myself humbly associated with the universe. I believe that my future life brings abundance from all sides and giving it a form materializes it.

Nature has accepted my appeal to its fullest satisfaction. "Every moment I will be moving towards big and bigger truths. My mind is calm, quiet, serene and idyllic. I offer this day to life freely and fearlessly." In return as a reward life gives me happiness and fulfilment in a measure much more splendorous. The benediction/blessings come in both expected and unexpected ways. The universe gives gifts in a surprising way unexpectedly. "I am really grateful to life. May my life continue its journey easily, simply, naturally, happily and comfortably", I say it to myself.

29

Abundance of Love

We have understood wrongly. We have come here to become the masters of a clean, unblemished, unrestricted love. We are the ones who have come from nature, the ones who will return to nature itself. We have come here to understand individual or personal love. There are different types of loves.

Universal love

Confused love

Sweat's love

Mad love

Shattered love

Complete love

Love has already become perfect in us now. It is to be caused to flow out. That's all. We have come here to become free and lovely human beings. Those who are in old memories there is no unrestricted love. Do stop telling that old story itself. Really there are no again and again adjectives. Love just says: "Exhibit or show love". Love more and more and love. Excel at that.

You shine in love, you laugh, weep, suffer pain, get healed up, fall down, get up and play again, do the work, do live, do die--do everything in love.

That much is enough! That love itself is abundance, wealth, happiness and continuous.

30

Favourable Reaction

Let the other people keep doing whatever the universe reacts to you personally. Though the policemen are there everywhere we can drive the car happily waving the hand to them or thinking that some trouble came we may get depressed or dejected.

It is not possible to control the acts of another person. Nevertheless you can control the acts of the universe and the people through your favourable reaction and response.

"Though the conditions and situations might be howsoever you can get happiness, joy, pleasure and wealths".

If we start living saying "All is well" life becoming ecstatic or supremely happy keeps on becoming blissful and excellent. Not only that much, if we focus on "All is well" we will influence the world around us. You becoming the palace of light you will appear to the universe like the guiding light or the light house which shows the right route to the ships. Really changing the world means being a model to others living in happiness, joy and pleasure, being useful to the people is the only way and the only option.

That how powerful is your light will not be known to you yourself. Every individual too who radiates powerful light to others without the electric power connection is more powerful than a million lights. Believe it or not the light which an individual radiates casts its influence over millions of the people. It is impossible for us even to imagine that.

31

Ego-Centric Personality Vs Soul–Centric Personality

There are people having two types of personalities in this world--ego-centric and soul-centric personalities. The ego-centric individual will be entangled in fear-based, struggle for existence type of ways, means and policies. Having been subjected to the control of the society's ways-means he will be undergoing the agony of the past emotional blows and pains. Thinking that the world itself is different and he himself is different, getting himself separated from the nature's network of life he turns away from the truth and all the natural joys, happinesses and pleasures of life. Depression, irritability, anger, dissatisfaction, intolerance, displeasure will always keep on dancing in him.

The prime difference between the ego-centric and the life-centric groups of individuals is the relation they have with their mind.

He who is soul-centred will be the one who is an endless, limitless ocean of love, merciful and the one who would very much enjoy life. He will be the one who leads his life following the nature's sacred intelligence which is very much within himself.

The ego-centric individual is the one who refuses to have anything with meditation, observing silence, selflessness, being fearless, humility or humbleness and remains the one who always keeps on murmuring and chattering about something or the other and at times for nothing! He will be the one who without taking deep rest, sound sleep, without having the love for nature who undergoes distress and grief having the mind producing the sound imitating the one made by jumping repeatedly from impatience, disappointment as children.

The soul-centric individual having been dead to the wounds of the past, coming out of the feelings of anger and scapegoat, will be experiencing the supreme peace of the heart, sacredness and humility or humbleness. Keeping on experiencing harmony, courteous behavior of sharing the emotions, thoughts and feelings of others sympathetically and unrestricted love with all the living beings collectively will be always emitting natural happiness in his face and in his life.

32

The Fear of Defeat

Mainly in businesses and elsewhere too the fear of possibly getting defeated is quite big. Its twin brother is the fear that one might get rejected. We all will keep on facing these two everyday in one way or the other. We all are the ones who get defeated in one way or the other. Even an Olympic champion too will have won after being defeated several times. But there will be a relative to defeat. Many a time it will be imaginary. Inside the inner mind itself the defeat will have taken place first.

We, instead of saying to ourselves that I failed, if we release and rectify that I won't repeat this mistake which is responsible for this defeat our state of mind will be different altogether. How seriously we think or cogitate about the defeat is left to us. The external fear gets converted into the internal fear while the internal fear gets converted into the external fear.

The fear created after suffering a defeat makes the mind to entertain the feeling that in future too it might result in yet another defeat; so let me not go to its affair at all. Goaded by this negative feeling the mind refuses to try again. Thus it is the unreal fears of the mind that throw away our sublime future into an unused and abandoned water-well.

Here the defeat is not one of importance. But deciding a retrial as being not at all required is the real defeat. From then on the devil of the fear of defeat won't leave at all.

33

The Right Choice

The most important lesson of life that all of us should learn is taking "right decisions". The irony is that none of us will have thought to take a wrong decision. Strangely a decision which is felt to be right today turns out to be wrong tomorrow for various reasons.

Some formula or rule of conduct which is not known to us will cause to make the right decision to be a wrong decision. Though howsoever we may try we will not make a wrong decision. Some one desire imbued with a bad purpose will instigate us to consume drinks, drugs, tobacco etc., in life in a peculiar way. Our body pumping the blood, causing the heart to beat, giving labour it teaches the lesson about how to live naturally. Nevertheless yielding to and coming under the spell of bad habits, becoming slaves to them and becoming lazy we lose the body's basic health. Though the serious decisions pertaining to studies, profession, marriage, buying property, settling in foreign countries making them as our base etc., are taken with due care after measuring, pouring and weighing the pros and cons feeling that they are the right decisions, subsequently the same decisions may be felt to be the wrong decisions in future. That moment's fascination, the desire inspire us to take those decisions. In life there are no wrong decisions, instead there are lessons to learn, that's all. If the lessons are observed properly our future life becomes full of joy, happiness, mirth and merriment.

Whenever and wherever we take a decision of fascination then wisdom becoming blind big-big pictures will not be seen. Inner guidance too is not heard. Generally we take these decisions of fascination through a series of rights and wrongs that happened in life. But after examining with the experts and conversing or having a dialogue with others, if we ask the question to the heart there won't be wrong decisions.

34

There are No Wrong Decisions

There are no wrong decisions. But after a decision is executed the mind sowing the seeds of suspicion and fear creates problems. This itself is the way we generally follow. If we walk in several ways we get lost, that's all. It is not just getting lost; life becomes confused, complicated and difficult to be understood.

On the basis of the decision it is of utmost importance to have better relationship. For example, after the marriage every day we should go on developing better relationship. Imagine what might happen if the wife grows suspicious about the husband and conversely the husband gets suspicious about the wife. "The sea of suspicion has no shores. He/she who embarks upon it is without a rudder and a compass." Close on the very heels of suspicion comes the fear. The biggest awareness means having our best relation first with ourselves and having our best relation with others afterwards. This is most important. We should not decide our method either under pressure or by fickleness or by oscillating on the swing of "to be" or "not to be"; "Whether to do' or 'not to do'. We must follow a middle path which neither gets stuck in a conflict between two opposing views or thoughts nor has too much of a self-confidence.

Mind will not have a clear cut idea of what it wants. Man always keeps on searching thoroughly for this, that and even for that which is unwanted. This eternal truth is very poignantly brought out in the following poem of D.V. Gundappa:

"Life is all thirst: for that, for this, for yet another.

Recalling power, wealth, beauty and fame.

The mind is boiling all the while Mankuthimma.

The duality of the right decision is naturally there for all human beings. Right from the highest desire which divinity inspires down to the decision which stands the test of a good decision "Is this desire good for me and to the society" taking that decision we should infuse the work-enthusiasm into the mind in such a way that it should perpetually engage itself in that task itself. Otherwise like the child having no awareness the mind keeps on pestering. The composition of every living being is to grow the biggest bumper spiritual crop and then distributing it to all the living beings. This is exactly what those who are worthy of universal respect and reverence did. Even now they have been doing it. Shall we also follow their footsteps?

35

There is Nothing Called Impossible

There are no diseases which are incurable, there is nothing which is impossible to achieve in the world. Those which are called impossible would be coming from the negatives only like I don't have the capacity, I might get afflicted with diseases, this task is not possible by me etc. The reason for this is the mind of poverty which without having relationship with abundance sees only the deficiencies. That is just keeping the mind in the confusions which are vague or not clear. There is nothing which is impossible to the mind. Many achievers and great souls have showed after achieving this in their lives. The word impossible is not at all found in their dictionary! If we do not make up our mind we cannot shake a grass straw or a blade of grass. If we make up our mind we can climb even the Himalayan mountain, we can carry out, perform, fulfil or cultivate any achievement too. We can do anything and everything. In short we can turn wonders!

Though many achievers who had physical disability, rather who were differently abled, like Hellen Keller, journalist Ved Mehta, Nobel Prize winner physicist Stephen Hawking, the blind woman Ashvini Angadi of Karnataka, Bachendripal who scaled the Himalayan mountain, Anuranima etc., after achieving great achievements have become bright and splendid examples. We too making up our mind do bigger achievements which are useful to us and to the society at large. Let us always do good deeds by the strength of being in good company, making good thought, good determination. If we are always imbued with fearlessness, the quality of not showing one's pride or haughtiness, selflessness and incessant enthusiasm we can achieve whatever we want. Instead of having the decisions which say it will never happen, fear, cynicism let us always have curiosity, kindness, courage and boldness and by doing so let us see to it that our respective dreams come true.

36

Supreme Wealth

Would you like to have the eight kinds of material wealth of a king...? If so always think of joy, happiness, love, compassion and abundance etc. In order to enable you to have abundance here are the lush green affirmations of abundance.

My income has always been increasing. Be it anywhere, whenever and whatever I will always create it by abundance.

Today is the day of supreme happiness. Money is coming flowing in both expected and unexpected paths.

Green flag having been shown to me to go ahead on my own self, I embrace the new happily.

I support others to become rich. In turn the life supports me to become rich in such a way that I am surprised myself.

I will respond positively and favourably with free will to the endless richness which is found everywhere.

The world I am living in is loving and friendly.

I am really grateful to everything and to everyone.

I have the capability or the worth of desiring the best. In short I deserve to desire the best. And I accept the best now itself.

All is well and I am safe.

37

Daily Affirmations

How shall we begin the day? What are the first thoughts that come in our mind the moment we get up in the morning? Do you blame yourself, the situations and the circumstances...? Will the fear as to what might happen this day, anxiety and suspicion pester you...?

As we begin the day so we live the whole day. When you get to see yourself in the mirror in the bathroom what do you say? While taking bath what do you think? While going to work from home, while sitting in the car, do you murmur saying 'this hopeless and desolate work' or do you go joyously......?

I suggest some affirmations to be said immediately after you get up.

Immediately after getting up let us express our gratitude to the bed saying 'Thank you bed, you gave me a happy sleep'.

Saying to yourself 'I love you darling so and so' you utter your name. You say to yourself that it is going to be a good day.

I am a big gift to the world.

Today wonderful experiences are waiting for me. Life loves me.

When you get up say this affirmation in the bath room. Let us say to ourselves: 'Happy morning darling, I Love you'.

Let us have a good day today.

If I am happy I am verily the magnet of miracles myself.

Today I have time for all works. I am looking handsome/beautiful.

The affirmations are only the starters or the beginning factors. They show the path.

Open the mind's eye, open the door of the heart. As the first step say these affirmations in the mind itself today, tomorrow and the whole week. Then observe how your life transforms itself for better. Let us affirm: Every thought I think today is shaping my future.

38

Character

To create the character that we want hundreds and thousands of choices take place. These choices by which you want to become whatever in future in order to build that personality they will continue to help towards that end. If this type of decisions are not there, you will become one common ordinary man among the crowd. You will be living, you will be there as a human being. But character will not have been built up in you.

Personality will not take place just like that without doing anything. Just as the sculptor gives several strokes to chisel the idol out of a stone, we too should cause to shape out the personality of character by being associated with good and virtuous persons, by entertaining good thoughts, by doing good deeds and virtuous actions, by thinking and pondering deeply, by reflecting and meditating and by good reading. Above all, conscious decision and conscious process are absolutely essential.

Personality is not something which comes by birth. It is not like the finger print which cannot be changed. Since the personality does not come by birth or through inheritance we should take the responsibility of building it up like a palatial building by placing one brick on the other.

Personality is determined on the basis of how do we react and respond to the incidents and events that take place in life.

The defeat or the winning of each game is determined by your personality. Whether you are going to be rich or you groan and murmur in poverty and dearth, how do you manage the difficult time-all these depend upon our personality.

Some virtues or good qualities will have to be embodied wisely and nurtured with faith, trust and making repeated earnest efforts. Just as a seed after sprouting, growing into a sapling and then into a tree, we will have to cause them to grow a little slowly and steadily moment by moment. The virtues will have to be grown by your sacred mind, by good heart and by courage. Just as a sculptor etches out and throws away that which is unnecessary in the statue we should etch out and remove the vices, bad habits and defects which are there in us.

If the desired personality should come in us, we should not only earn these qualities but also strengthen them. Every day after welcoming them with jubilance and effectiveness, achieving our goal, we should distribute them to others too.

If the virtuous personality is applied to the works, if the challenges are accepted that task becoming successfully fulfilled the works will become stable and permanent. When once we build our personality rightly and well that becoming a strong and firm foundation builds the palatial building of life of our ambitions. The power of causing to complete our lifetime of a hundred years fruitfully is in the virtuous character.

39

Not Just Living; Contribute, Contribute

The right work of men is not just being in existence; they should cause the life to be a light. Generally for the most part we will be spending our life like the pilot machine of a self-driven aeroplane. Wasting the days doing the same movement and acts of monotony we spend the charmless days. We all like a comfortable and a pleasant life. Comfortable life without hard and sincere work and physical exertion to the body and mind is a life of betrayal of trust and hence a treacherous life which is not right and fair is contrary to justice. But it is just the life of a living dead achieving nothing though spending years of time. At last at the end of life only repentance and worry that I didn't achieve anything will remain. It is therefore better to die for something rather than live for nothing!

If we should really live, we should experience and enjoy life by living it. The life which is found only once should be enjoyed to the hilt with ecstasy or supreme happiness. It is not just being in existence and living superficially without any use we should dive deep into its depth. Of what avail it is if one claims that "I am alive because I am not dead"? Therefore coming out of the mechanical dreariness and monotony of life we should always savour the taste of the sweetness of life being ever lively.

40

Linking of Living and Non-Living

In this world every living being with all the living network the inert matter with the conscious being, the conscious being with the non-living matter are all mutually knitted together. Here there is no separate existence to anybody and any thing/matter. This intelligence of nature is perfect. In order to build our grand future we should follow virtuous principles every moment responsibly, tread the right path and perform good deeds.

Your future is to be created on a big canvas which is as wide as this sky with varied colours drawing one line after the other. You yourself should create this grand, colourful and beautiful picture of your gigantic future according to your will and wish. The depth of the quality of involving actively in this work is beyond measure and endless. The production of the beautiful picture of a model personality will not happen accidentally either in our life or in our mind. Even accidents too will have somehow after getting constructed passed through the mind. We are really in an eternal world in which 'everything is possible". If tried like a painter who draws pictures or a sculptor who sculpts a statue imagining something it is definitely possible to materialize what one has conceived as a dream or what one has felt.

The very last sculptor of my life is none other than myself. One powerful difficulty in knowing and celebrating that this power is in all of us naturally itself is total loss of memory. That is very much always within us only. That is verily the illusion called "I am different/separate". Should not forget that I too am an atom of nature. Forgetting that I am God myself, I am of divine origin we invite the devil called "I" to be present in us without our knowledge. Fighting and fighting for name, fame, sex, selfishness and power and wealth throughout life, living speaking foolishly, nonsensically and uselessly and breathing the last is an useless and a good for nothing life.

The beliefs, opinions and ideas of division and discrimination having been injected and indoctrinated into us by the society, bad books, elders, why only that much they having been ingrained in our genes since millions of years to the extent of overflowing we have become the centres of ego. Similarly out of 780 crore people only a few lakhs of people after attaining liberation becoming life-centred have finally become great souls free from worldly obligations, relations, attachments etc.

Allama's (A great seer of Karnataka) vachana's meaning

Clearly points out that in the forest called our body five dead bodies called lust, anger, infatuation, arrogance and jealousy have fallen down. These very dead bodies pestering those who are around us and our relatives too the group becomes bigger. These five bodies never ever get consumed completely by fire and the forest too never ever gets used. That is why there is the fruitfulness of man's life if he gets released from the five dead bodies.

We, being unaware of the infinite divine power which is very much present within ourselves only, are throwing the life's oil called the time in the sand every moment. The biggest illusion that is found in all of us is the ego. The widest and the truest immortality is 'I'. This is the actual truth. All our thoughts are only limited concepts. Even when the immortal and infinite thoughts come they too are concepts only and are not the actuals.

All our thoughts having been filled with ego, even its external face too being ego, it illudes or imagines that verily I am the powerful being who can create this, that and what all.

Quit of blaming and criticising the others. Perhaps this itself is the biggest hole the total destruction of men's power.

We judging ourselves, judging the others, finding out faults in them amounts to throwing away our power or energy and the energy waves into the garbage uselessly. Each one is on their own path of 'nirvana' or salvation and the divine power has been protecting them.

All of us are getting the necessary life-experience and we are reaching the highest peak of the spiritual power. We should reserve our prime powers for love, gratitude, relatedness and joys only but not for making judgements and for finding faults or for getting ourselves separated from others.

Don't be harsh and tough about yourself. Instead of blaming yourself and others you better forgiveness. For all of us intimacy, love, affection and relations are most important. That which is called compassion is the best response which is present in us. That always empowers or strengthens us and others.

The more and more we send more agreeableness, patience and love to the universe the more extensive becomes the horizon of our consciousness. Instead of judgement it is the consent, love, compassion which apart from bringing out what is best in us their power will be made available for the division of the earth-the continents. The change of powers inside us causes the change of the powers of the division of the earth.

41

The Divinely Intelligent Universe

We are in a divinely intelligent universe. There are powers of intelligence all around us. Science says in its physics laboratories that the construction of the universe is built by the waves of intelligent, tiny atoms of consciousness.

The most important fact is that all the living beings are closely knitted together in this intimate network. Everything of this universe is perfectly, intimately constructed with everything else and everyone very intelligently. It is not possible to construct by anybody else better than this. Not at all possible. We are really specially fortunate enough. Today we have incarnated here in a body which is associated with mind.

42

Stepping Forward or Stepping Backward

We either move forward positively or move backward negatively. We will never be stagnant. Either we grow or we die. The moment we retire we will become like the ones who are dead. But life's supreme purpose is creation, ever creative and ever active. The people after retirement will stop living and creating. That is why the retired persons die too early after their retirement.

Since they forget the very purpose of their life in the universe their inner consciousness puts an end to their physical life. The people join work to retire and dying without living without being lively is madness, pure and simple. Such people are so fond of death that they run half-way to meet it!

Amassing money and wealth for post-retirement life too is an illusion. To say that we will live happily according to our will and wish too is an illusion only. The happiness of the freedom of life which begins from the first day itself and which could be enjoyed even after one's retirement should be enjoyed now itself. Life is there in the joys, happinesses and pleasures of each and every moment and each and every day.

If we choose and do only those works which give us the most enjoyment then the work instead of becoming a bore becomes a play. If this truth is realized very well we will become absolutely free.

43

When There is No Ego God Descends in Me

When ego is dissolved the God enters me and the divine acts take place.

Beyond the mountain's valley a stream of the waves of sounds kept on flowing. This was surprising to all. The elders of the town had never ever heard such a sound wave. At last an youth deciding that he should know what is that by going down the mountain went there. Over there dozens together of people queued up in a line of turn were engaged in the work--some were carrying stones on their head, some others were cutting and carving the stones with chisels to make statues, still some others were engaged in erecting the stones neatly. This youth going near a worker over there asked him: "What are you doing?" Murmuring he sorrowfully said that till he gets another job this work was inevitable for him and that was why he was doing that work.

The youth then asked the second worker: "What are you doing?" He said: "I am earning money for the sake of my family." Then the youth asked the same question to the third one too. He replied: "I am sculpting a beautiful statue". The youth asked the same question to yet another worker.

He replied that he was constructing a residential school for the orphans. Further on the youth questioned a woman. She said: "we are constructing a school for the facility of the present and the future generations of this city, for the poor and the orphan children". Expressing wonder saying "Very good" the youth questioned another: "What about you, Sir?" He said that he was striving to provide education in order to eradicate the ignorance and poverty of all the generations through this work. I am in the process of knowing myself." Lastly the youth asked the same question to an elderly person who was smiling brimming with joy. He laughing with a loud laugh said: "The ego in me has melted away in God many years ago itself. In order to say that I have done anything I am not at all there myself." He concluded saying that God getting his work done through this body has been causing to do the work of awakening all the people.

44

Patience

Be peaceful, calm and quiet in the event that is going on here and now at this moment. Our grasping world begins right from where we are at this moment and not in the dream we might reach some time in future. Instead of hurriedly jumping to the decisions much before time trust your beliefs strongly. Do not accept defeat quickly. In order to enjoy the beautiful rewards which life really gives it is neither necessary that we should make a compromise with the old life values nor we should ignore or neglect our feelings and desires.

Patience means it is one getting deeply and devoutly engrossed putting one's heart and soul in the process of the task on one's hand. It is like waiting till the bud blossoms into a flower. It is like simply waiting a butterfly coming out of the state of a caterpillar on its own, it is not doing damage, disaster or great loss to oneself by hastening or hurrying. Discern the wisdom in the sayings "Haste makes waste" and "Married in haste and repented at leisure." The real patience is certainly not keeping on grinding one's teeth together in anger saying to oneself that I will tolerate for another five minutes. Afterwards all these troublesome or embarrassing situations getting over and good happens.

Patience does not mean bearing with or tolerating impatience, discontent or dissatisfaction and disappointment. **Instead it is going on increasing our strength from each and every incident we faced.** If that situation expects certain acts you should definitely perform them.

Patience does not mean being immobile or immobility. It is not being completely satisfied either. Instead it is dedicating or offering myself to the process of climbing a very high mountain. Coming face to face with the truths that come on the way as different types of waves one after the other. During the day there will be some waiting incidents. For example: you phone up somebody. They won't receive it. A bus, a train or a friend does not come at the appointed time. Then the consciousness of our patience should get awakened observing without boiling with impatience, intolerance, developing patience, instead of running away from what is we should breathe slowly. That means we should experience the penance of patience.

'No penance (tapas) other than patience'

Let us always follow the following eternal truth of patience said by saint Vadiraja;

Wait wait O mind wait

Wait till the planted sapling grows and yields fruit.

Wait till the packed up food is there to eat in future

Wait instead of getting perturbed when difficulty comes

Bear the rude and unkind words uttered by the wicked men.

Wait till the water is put to the boiling milk.

It is not enough saying to yourself as to how the grand future's plans should be. You should keep on doing some necessary works for them today itself. If even in old age health should be better let the exercise which should be done right from now, walking and food be proper. May be it is companion's slow walking, the reaching of post may be slow, when saying to ourselves that they are neglecting us, when that which is wanted does not come to memory, when concentration of attention becoming difficult--on many such happenings doing what is right at that moment itself is patience.

Instead of saying or seeing "what is wrong" raking up the past history to see "who is wrong" we will have been dead to what we should necessarily do at this moment, here and now. Making the weapon of patience our strength, keeping on increasing our strength for our good purpose we should complete the work we have taken up.

45

Gratitude

Let us be grateful to this today.

To the cinemas which made me elated with joy, to the telephone which helped communicate with the people.

To your computer and

to the electricity which lights up the

whole house, which makes several

instruments and equipments to move,

to the bus, train and aeroplanes,

to the roads, to the orderly system of

traffic lights,

to those who have built the bridges,

to the dog, to the cat, to the child, to

the dearly loved, beloveds,

to the eyes which read this,

to your imagination, to your thoughts,

to your words/talks, to your laugh and

to your smiles let us be thankful.

Let us be grateful for being alive, for breathing.

For we being we, for living let us be grateful.

Just two words can change the life--

"Thanks, thanks".

46

Our Transformation Can Be Caused By Our Morality

The act of transformation takes place vibrantly within our mind. There are wonderful powers in all of us. We all expect better results for our efforts. Most among us are ready to pay the price of hard work or labour which success and happiness demand. Nevertheless we expect result from the intensity of our power and will. But still the quality of the results of our power and the intensity of will is dependent on only one thing and that is our morale.

Generally the people exert their influence on us by dumping their negativities on us. The media, society and the elders unintentionally would keep on exerting their influence on us without they being aware of it. But if only none of us surrenders our morale and the mental attitude to them their influences would do nothing to us. None can "enrage us to become angry". We surrender ourselves to anger. If we lose our morale somebody having done something to us becomes irrelevant. We ourselves are the choosers. Gandhiji said: "Nobody can hurt or inflict pain to me without my permission. That is not possible at all". They just test our morale. We will get accustomed to opposition, anger, intolerance, jealousy or suspicions, cynicism and fear which shake us easily. We fail in the test of patience.

If we belittle ourselves that we are unfit or good for nothing then again we fail in the examination of morale. If we have any concern about ourselves, we only will have to bear the complete responsibility of our mental attitudes. We should instead of always getting our morale lowered or lessened shun the path of past time which leads us to the ditch of depression, take to the path of self-confidence which enhances the morale. The prime choice of posing strong belief in future which is absolutely essential to mankind is morale. It is a very big asset for us; a highly valuable huge wealth. That is precisely why it should be safeguarded well.

That which is a wealth of this kind, which brightens the future and which is a positive attitude is one of the fundamental factors of success. All of us having personal principle, theory, moral principles, restraints, discipline and a positive attitude about ourselves is essential. If we develop our inner power abundantly it will be helpful to have success and happiness in all the fields of life. We should guard ourselves against the thieves and the wicked people called the negative thoughts which rob us by being around us only.

47

The Power of Being Lively and Enthusiastic

What all we can do in life.

What all we can build.

For that we being lively and cheerful is most important.

Kuvempu has said that "Pat with your palm and wake up the ones who are like dead, cause to sit those who quarrel over small matters and cause them to love each other, cause to pour tears profusely to jealousy, express your good wishes in a solemn way for all to live together." Kuvempu wished India to be a garden of peace of all nationalities. It is therefore, of utmost importance to realize that life is the supreme power.

In the breath of everyday, every moment we get either more of abundance or more of poverty. In the breathing of every day we can either become healthy persons or like the ones who are aged and infirm. Every day we travel either towards death or towards immortality. But life is not a noun. It is a verb. It is a movement. It is action or an act of doing something, an act of ever moving.

Health, ill health, more joyful or sorrowful today than yesterday--all these are there in our thought, word and acts. This is verily our own decision. We ourselves are the ones who have to decide. If we are to make the good use of the power of life we should be prompt and honest unto ourselves. We should act in accordance with our thoughts. We should walk our talk. Transform the thoughts into power through acts. In order to utilise the power of feelings live responsibly. Life's all power is ingrained in responsibility. Observe all around, you will find that there is power here, there and everywhere. If we make some one else stronger and more powerful and richer we too will become more powerful in the process. By turning your face towards life, by being pro-life you will enjoy the power of life, you will follow it too.

48

Wealth Abundance

Money and abundance in life won't come without strenuous effort or labour or by the help of others. If only when the consistent and continuous thoughts of abundance are presented to the universe in the form of action the abundance of money comes.

If we train up our thoughts slowly to go towards positive expectations, if I say to myself that I am fit, useful and deserving and my acts too are likewise so and the abundance of money is coming for the good of all of us, then the floods of possibilities and good ideas will flow in torrents in our heart. The words and talks of curiosity and enthusiasm will come together and assemble around us. Influential persons and the ones having money will come searching for you and meet you. The demand quite equal to our intense will or desire coming in the market opportunities, money, abundance will all come in plenty on their own.

You keeping on seeing all this with awe and getting wonderstruck, enjoying how once in the past all that which was impossible to your hand is now within the reach of your hand naturally, will come to know that these attractions, experiences are the ones which have come naturally and not by your struggle.

If you are excited from joy and are bewildered seeing this abundance coming beforehand itself without evidence and bases then they will really come and be visible to you.

Karuna Jeeva Kalyana Trust in action--Its working style of social service

Every month 20 water tanks of animals and birds are being kept throughout the city. In Davangere, Harihar, Ranebennur, Haveri, Shivamogga, Chitradurga, Channagiri, Jagalur and elsewhere too the water tanks for drinking purpose have been kept.

Every year 2000 saplings are being planted and protected throughout the city.

Every year during summer free butter milk and water are being distributed for 1 month at four places in the city.

Karuna Jeeva Kalyana Trust in action--Its working style of social service

For the post-SSLC poor girl students we have been giving a financial assistance of Rs. 10,000/ – per student per year for their education. Besides, for selected poor schools teaching materials, note books and uniforms are being supplied.

Creating awareness programme and the personality development programmes meant for the teen-aged girls are being conducted in schools and colleges.

Karuna Jeeva Kalyana Trust in action--Its working style of social service

On the second Sunday of every month conducting a health check-up camp medical treatment sufficient enough for 1 month for one patient is being caused to be given. By now we have already organised 210 check-up camps.

For a bad-habit-free India in order to create awareness among the youth about the intoxicating things like Gutka, tobacco, alcoholic liquors etc., different posters are being got printed and pasted and several people awareness programmes are being conducted.

Karuna Jeeva Kalyana Trust in action--Its working style of social service

Push carts are being distributed to the widows and the poor women selling vegetables, fruits and the like. By now already 170 carts have been distributed.

Karuna Jeeva Kalyana Trust in action--Its working style of social servic

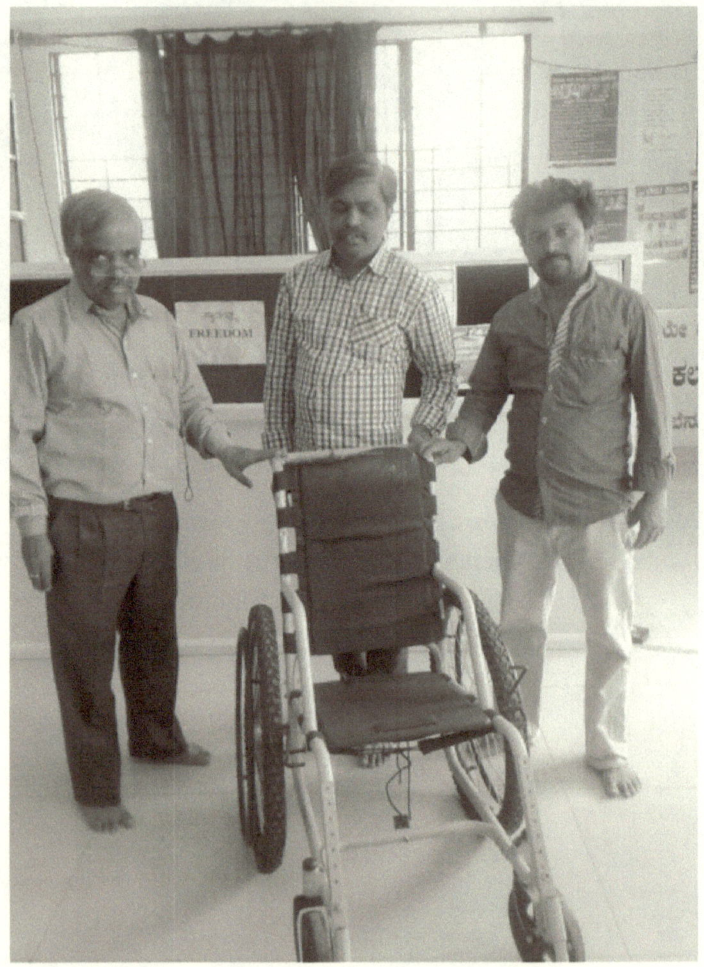

By giving the necessary and useful assistance to the orphans, differently-abled persons, women, weaker persons, aged persons, physically weak persons commensurate with its capacity the Trust has been rendering real social service incessantly.

Karuna Jeeva Kalyana Trust in action--Its working style of social service

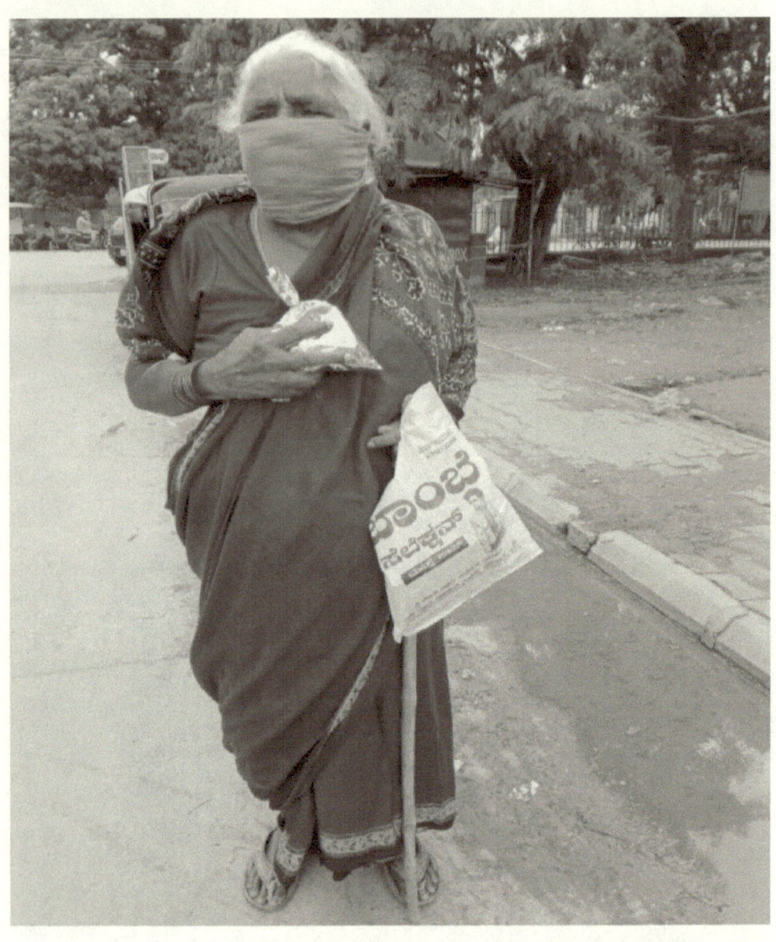

By giving the necessary and useful assistance to the orphans, differently-abled persons, women, weaker persons, aged persons, physically weak persons commensurate with its capacity the Trust has been rendering real social service incessantly.

Karuna Jeeva Kalyana Trust in action--Its working style of social service

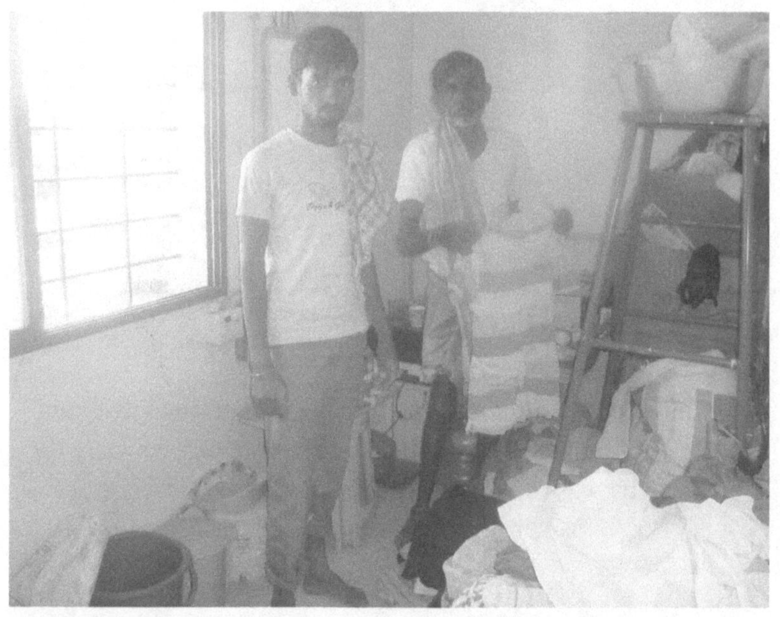

Every day collecting old clothes and old articles they are being distributed among the poor people.

With the intention of making Davangere a place of drinking water drinking water tanks are being kept in places where the public go by walk in large numbers, in medical stores, grocery shops etc.,

To the traders who do their business sitting under the scorching sunshine 100 big umbrellas have been distributed

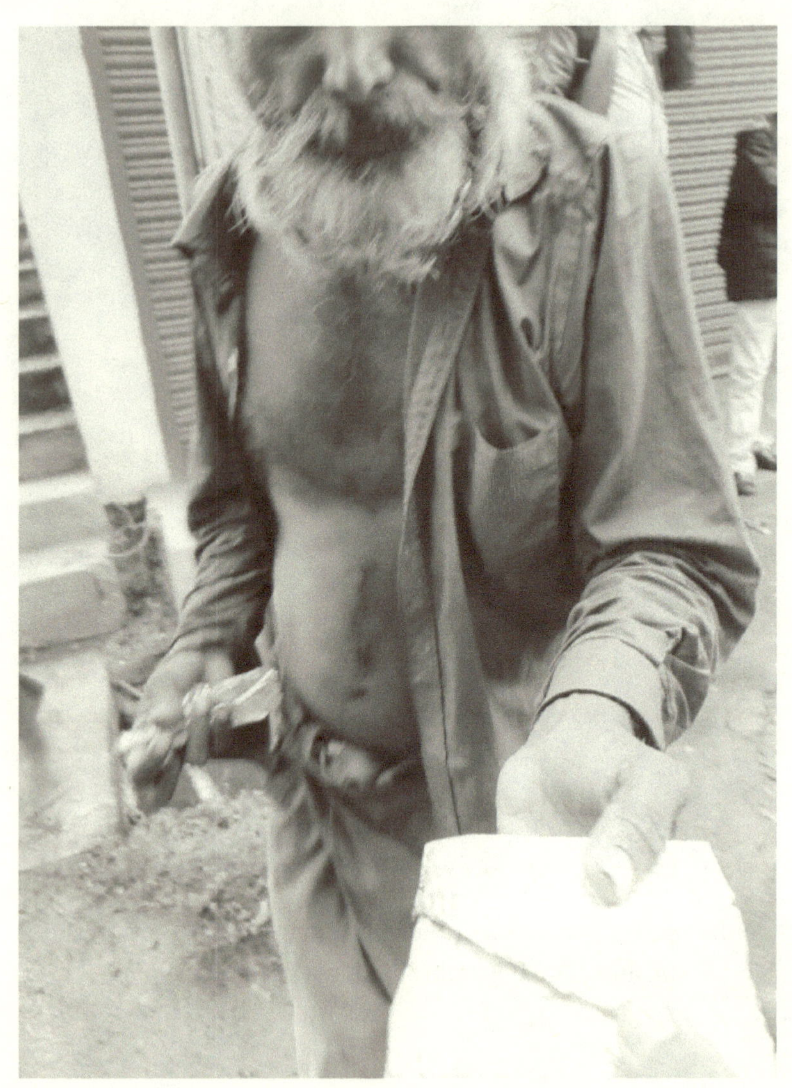

Every day for 50 poor people in Davangere, Harihar, Ranebennur and elsewhere one meal arrangement at a single division of the day like either morning or afternoon or night is being made.

Distribution of bicycles for underprivileged labourers to get to work

An humble and a polite request

After reading the matters presented in this book one, two or any number per day we follow them in our life we will observe how we get its reward experimentally.

I pray that may mother nature bless you, the reader, and your family with ever increasing "supreme happiness, supreme love, supreme health, supreme peace and supreme fruitfulness".

"May there be people's welfare, world's welfare and all living beings welfare"

– Shivanakere Basavalingappa
Karuna Jeeva Kalayana Trust (Regd)
3rd Main Road, 3rd Cross,
Mama's Joint Road, MCC 'B' Block,
Davangere-577004. Mobile: No. 9886645880

Shivanakere Basavalingappa

Karuna Jeeva Kalyana Trust (Regd)

DAVANGERE.

The book **"Wisdom for Life: A Journey of Abundance, Peace, Happiness and Fulfillment"** which dear friend Sri Basavalingappa has collected from different sources is a thoughtful handbook that builds up and gives the love of life besides filling the zest of life. At the end of this book he has explained the pro-life programmes of his organization 'Karuna Jeeva Kalyana Trust". He has laid down an ideal which is a model for others that it is not enough if good words are spoken, that should come to be seen in action too. Just as the sanctity or purity of purpose that lies behind a work determines the effect of that work the sanctity or purity that lies behind this book shapes the reading minds.

"Walk the talk" or that one's conduct should be in tune with one's word is the common expectation. Acting in tune with what one says is said to be 'Dharma'. But more often than not there are occasions when this will end up in words only. But the articles of Basavalingappa's this book are the words which have risen from deeds. Action gives strength to the words which one speaks. That being what it is it is not possible to consider these words lightly as the words heard somewhere, spoken by someone. When word and deed become one 'that which is called word becomes Jyothirlinga' (the linga conceived as the concrete form of the Supreme Light). That which is called whosoever's word becomes verily my own.

In the complicated and perplexed condition of everyday in the uphill path of defeat and winning, the inspiration alone which does not know what defeat is can stand by being light to us. In this book there are words which are helpful to develop introspection to see the source of inspiration of this kind in ourselves only and the quality of putting in tireless efforts till the goal is reached. There are good words here about the importance of compassion-sympathies, help, forgiveness. Behind the statement that "Let alone forgiving others, first forgive yourselves" the awareness of deep psychology is working. On the whole there are words which help solve the complex problems of human relations which are faced by all in the journey of life. If these words are to be made our own self-effort is absolutely essential. I wish that may this book be a beacon light to those who undergo the trauma and torments, the trials and sufferings in the vicissitudes of life.

– G.S. Jayadeva,
Deenabhandhu Trust,
Chamarajanagar.

www.ingramcontent.com/pod-product-compliance
Lightning Source LLC
LaVergne TN
LVHW041039150826
845672LV00001B/384

* 9 7 9 8 8 9 4 4 6 3 9 5 7 *